ESSENTIAL

MOVI
E-BUSINESS

STEVE SLEIGHT

A Dorling Kinders

000143739

Dorling DK Kindersley

LONDON, NEW YORK, SYDNEY, DELHI, PARIS
MUNICH, & JOHANNESBURG

Senior Designer Jamie Hanson
DTP Designer Julian Dams, Amanda Peers
Production Controller Michelle Thomas

Managing Editor Adèle Hayward
Senior Managing Editor Stephanie Jackson
Senior Managing Art Editor Nigel Duffield

Produced for Dorling Kindersley by

studio cactus C

13 SOUTHGATE STREET   WINCHESTER   HAMPSHIRE   SO23 9DZ

Editor Kate Hayward
Designer Laura Watson

First published in Great Britain in 2001 by
Dorling Kindersley Limited,
9 Henrietta Street,
Covent Garden, London WC2E 8PS

2 4 6 8 10 9 7 5 3 1

Copyright © 2001 Dorling Kindersley Limited
Text copyright © 2001 Steve Sleight

A CIP catalogue record for this book is available
from the British Library

ISBN 0 7513 1215 0

Reproduced by Colourscan, Singapore
Printed in Hong Kong by Wing King Tong Co. Ltd.

See our complete catalogue at
www.dk.com

CONTENTS

INTRODUCTION

The fast-changing digital world demands a new approach to the way we structure our businesses and interact with our customers. Managers must be ready to embrace new technologies and redefine strategies so that their organizations are able to adapt to the continuing rate of change. Moving to E-Business will show you how to integrate your systems, and those of your business partners, so that you can offer the best products and services to your customers. Practical advice, including 101 concise tips, will help you put e-business into practice and a self-assessment test at the end of the book allows you to evaluate your readiness for the challenge. As you embrace e-business practices within your organization, this book will be an invaluable source of reference and advice.

PREPARING FOR E-BUSINESS

The benefits of e-business have led to fundamental changes in the way business is organized and conducted. Prepare your organization to face the challenge and build a foundation for e-business.

DEFINING E-BUSINESS

The business world is continually being transformed by Information Technology (IT). Understand the implications of e-business, learn to see the possibilities new technologies bring to business strategies, and challenge existing strategic assumptions.

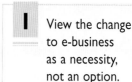

1 View the change to e-business as a necessity, not an option.

AN E-BUSINESS STRUCTURE

INTEGRATED NETWORKS
Data shared across organization

MULTIPLE SALES CHANNELS
Service channels are integrated

CUSTOMER VALUE
Consistent customer satisfaction

WHAT IS E-BUSINESS?

E-business stands for electronic business. It describes an organization that exploits the full potential of Information Technology (IT) to streamline its operations, with the aim of delivering the best possible value to the customer. E-business is not the same as e-commerce (electronic commerce); it is an extension of it. Crucially, e-business emphasizes the need to provide the same efficiency and value to the customer across all sales channels, not just on-line transactions via a Web site. Re-think your structure and begin to integrate all your systems into a cohesive whole.

Looking at Strategies

E-business relies on the development of new business strategies based on networks. The world has become increasingly inter-connected via digital computer and telecommunication networks. These offer fast, flexible, and cost-effective ways of doing business. Seek out new opportunities ahead of your competitors, and devise new business strategies that take advantage of this changing world.

Challenging Old Assumptions

Past business models were developed in a world where a person or organization communicated one-way with many others at the same time, for example, through television advertising. The customer relationship devolved, at best, to the sales teams and, at worst, to distributors, agents, and independent retailers. Now that global networks have the ability to carry high volumes of data, you can move your emphasis to target audiences directly via interactive media.

2 Challenge your existing business assumptions.

3 Identify ways to use new technology effectively.

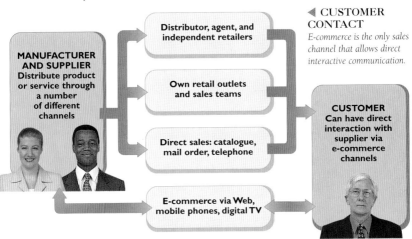

◀ CUSTOMER CONTACT
E-commerce is the only sales channel that allows direct interactive communication.

MANUFACTURER AND SUPPLIER
Distribute product or service through a number of different channels

Distributor, agent, and independent retailers

Own retail outlets and sales teams

Direct sales: catalogue, mail order, telephone

E-commerce via Web, mobile phones, digital TV

CUSTOMER
Can have direct interaction with supplier via e-commerce channels

UNDERSTANDING E-BUSINESS

Any organization wanting to survive in the newly interconnected business world must embrace e-business. Prepare to compete and learn to be forward-thinking so that your business stays ahead of competitors and retains existing customers.

4 Work at changing fear of the future to excitement at new opportunities.

COMPETING TO SUCCEED

The pace of business change has increased dramatically. Ensure that your organization has a clear vision of the digital future. Educate your team members to identify changes in markets due to the developing digital economy. Accept that the current changes are only the start of a business revolution that is likely to be as significant as the invention of the telephone.

Research and understand new technologies

Browse Internet to pinpoint new markets

◀ **KEEPING AHEAD**
Study advances in e-business and technology so that you are in a position to embrace the future.

TAKING NEW COMPETITORS SERIOUSLY

Do not allow yourself to become complacent about the size of your organization. In the change to e-business, new entrants often have an advantage over larger, more inflexible competitors. They have the freedom to implement new integrated IT systems designed for e-business. Work fast to identify and build on your organization's strengths and eliminate its weaknesses. Aim to prevent faster competitors from overtaking you.

POINTS TO REMEMBER

● New competitors often have more flexible structures and are able to adapt swiftly and efficiently to change.

● New businesses can design their processes from scratch to suit digital markets.

● It is important to stay receptive to new challenges and be willing to step into the unknown.

RETAINING CUSTOMERS

E-Business is about harnessing IT systems and fast networks to focus your efforts on identifying and satisfying your customers' needs and wants. Never before have customers had so much choice of products, services, and suppliers. This choice can be exercised through digital networks that offer instant access to information for comparative decision-making and purchasing. Your competitors may come from anywhere in the world. The message is clear. Put your customers first so that they remain your customers.

 5 Remember that organizations of all sizes can sell products cost-effectively anywhere in the world.

CULTURAL DIFFERENCES

Because e-business developed first in the US alongside the growth in the Internet, the language and culture of e-commerce and e-business has been dominated by the use of English and western commercial values. As e-business becomes ever more pervasive, consider delivering your electronic communication in different languages and cultural styles to hone your approach to markets or suppliers in other countries.

RECOGNIZING OPPORTUNITIES AND THREATS

OPPORTUNITIES	THREATS
Building closer relationships with your customers.	Losing your customers to new entrants or faster-moving competitors offering more efficient services.
Cutting costs caused by inefficient supply, service, and sales.	Finding your markets disappear completely, for example, because of changing technologies.
Receiving direct customer feedback and communication.	Finding internal inertia or politics prevent you making the necessary changes demanded by your customer.
Recognizing a new market niche out of changing customer demands.	Making wrong decisions about new technology and increasing costs.
Reacting faster and being more responsive than your competitors.	Being paralyzed by an inability to understand changes and fear of making wrong decisions.

MOVING TOWARDS E-BUSINESS

Converting to e-business is a complex process. It requires the conversion of existing processes and IT systems to suit new business strategies. Understand the changing value of knowledge and learn about the technology that supports e-business.

6 Identify the stage you have reached on the route to e-business.

7 Provide customers and suppliers with real-time data.

8 Aim to move and share information effectively.

HOW DID E-BUSINESS DEVELOP?

The rise of the Internet quickly gave birth to e-commerce, as suppliers and customers realized the cost and time benefits of on-line transactions. Greater efficiencies were also gained when on-line systems were applied throughout an organization's supply chain. Having an electronic shop-front on the Web, linked and constantly updated (real-time) to back-office information systems, led to the real challenge of e-business – providing audiences with up-to-date data through every sales channel.

VALUING KNOWLEDGE

With the increasing lack of differentiation in features, quality, or price of products and services, the ability to move and share information can be more valuable than the product itself. Recognize that, in the digital world, the ease with which information can be shared has radically changed the start-to-finish process (or value chain) that creates products and services. A niche has arisen for information intermediaries, or "infomediaries".

▲ **SHARING INFORMATION**
Digital technologies provide the crucial ability to quickly share real-time and accurate information, such as in the fast pace of this air control tower.

HARNESSING TECHNOLOGY

The revolution in changing markets is technology-driven. New telecommunication and IT networks and applications offer the ability for truly interactive, global communication. Work hard to maintain understanding of the changing technologies so that you are able to make strategic decisions for a technology-led world. Make it a fundamental part of your strategy to increase your organization's knowledge of relevant technology through recruitment and continuous training.

QUESTIONS TO ASK YOURSELF

Q Do I work to keep up-to-date with new technology, so that I can form effective strategies?

Q Do I rely on IT experts, rather than learning about new and developing technologies myself?

Q Do I have staff with the appropriate awareness of new and future technologies?

TYPICAL ROUTE TO E-BUSINESS

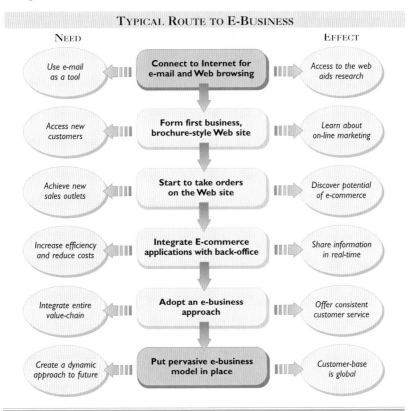

NEED		EFFECT
Use e-mail as a tool	**Connect to Internet for e-mail and Web browsing**	Access to the web aids research
Access new customers	**Form first business, brochure-style Web site**	Learn about on-line marketing
Achieve new sales outlets	**Start to take orders on the Web site**	Discover potential of e-commerce
Increase efficiency and reduce costs	**Integrate E-commerce applications with back-office**	Share information in real-time
Integrate entire value-chain	**Adopt an e-business approach**	Offer consistent customer service
Create a dynamic approach to future	**Put pervasive e-business model in place**	Customer-base is global

DEVELOPING AN E-BUSINESS STRATEGY

In a digital economy, you must be ready for a future of continual change. Re-examine your vision for the future, work closely with your staff, suppliers, and partners to implement change, and learn to view your organization from the customer's perspective.

9 Be prepared to question accepted business practices and methods.

10 Consider that the markets for your products or services are potentially global.

REDEFINING YOUR VISION

Look at new and future potential and redefine your business vision. In the global business environment, barriers to trade and the movement of capital are rapidly disintegrating due to digital technologies. Recognize that markets can increasingly be reached electronically, without significant cost or access barriers. Understand that you have more freedom to explore new opportunities, but so do your competitors.

WORKING INCLUSIVELY

The need to share and collaborate in defining future strategy is one of the first steps in moving to e-business. Involve your staff, suppliers, partners, and customers in redefining the vision for the future and your subsequent business strategy. Rethink your attitude to sharing information, and work with your colleagues to identify the types of information that should be shared so that your working relationships are more efficient.

11 Think of new ways to work with your partners.

▼ **IDENTIFYING CHANGE**
To identify and implement change successfully, aim to involve staff, partners, and customers by educating, enthusing, and empowering them to be actively involved.

Educate ⟹ **Enthuse** ⟹ **Empower**

BECOME YOUR OWN CUSTOMER

The focus of e-business must always be on the customer. The technology and the business structure follow on from, and are defined by, your vision of the value you intend to provide to your customers. Start by analyzing existing and future customers' needs and desires. Use your knowledge of your market to consider how customers' expectations will change in the future. This exercise can tell you more about your business than many far more costly initiatives.

FOCUSING ON CUSTOMER NEEDS ▼

Take a hard look at your organization from a customer's perspective. Services that keep the customer satisfied will ultimately benefit your organization.

DEVELOPING A STRATEGY

Focus on your customers and define them into groups

↓

Identify the needs and desires of each group

↓

Define the best process to deliver value to the customer

↓

Examine your existing structure to identify necessary changes

CUSTOMER BENEFITS

Receives prompt and helpful service

Develops confidence in organization

Specific needs are satisfied and met

BUSINESS BENEFITS

Attracts customers from competitors

Maintains customer loyalty

Increases market share

DO'S AND DON'TS

✔ Do implement procedures for sharing information.

✔ Do encourage your staff and colleagues to put customers first.

✘ Don't hold "strategic" information back from staff.

✘ Don't encourage hierarchical attitudes in your organization.

12 Take every opportunity to study competitors' strategies.

BUILDING A FOUNDATION FOR E-BUSINESS

Your e-business should be built on the solid foundation of fast, flexible, and integrated systems and good business relationships. Share your vision with your team, develop strategic partnerships, and take important decisions about technology.

 13 Make sure your entire management team shares the same vision.

 14 Empower teams to promote e-business developments.

EMPOWERING A TEAM ▼
Create an e-business team that is focused on identifying and solving e-business development issues and on championing your organization's transformation efforts.

SHARING THE VISION

Your staff can become so involved in the day-to-day running of existing processes that little time is left to focus on the more far-reaching changes that are required for e-business. However, developing an e-business strategy is a complex procedure, so it is essential that the entire management team and their staff understand and accept the strategic vision. Share the e-business strategy broadly within your organization and empower your staff to contribute to the process of change.

Customer-services Manager offers input

Managing Director chairs meeting

IT Manager offers technical viewpoint

Sales Manager presents sales perspective

Business Manager collates ideas

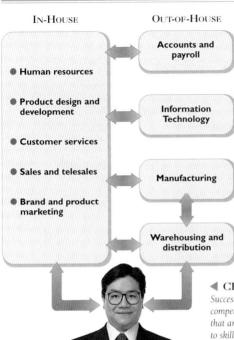

IN-HOUSE

OUT-OF-HOUSE

- Human resources
- Product design and development
- Customer services
- Sales and telesales
- Brand and product marketing

Accounts and payroll

Information Technology

Manufacturing

Warehousing and distribution

CUSTOMER

BUILDING PARTNERSHIPS

It is important to realize that you cannot be good at everything. The use of outsourcing has grown steadily as organizations, driven by a need to lower costs, have moved cost centres to outside specialists. Electronic business communities (EBCs) bring together skilled partners who collaborate to deliver excellent products and services to a global market. Develop the ability to enter and leave flexible partnerships when changing market conditions require it.

◀ **CREATING PARTNERSHIPS**
Successful organizations focus on their core competencies. They outsource other functions that are not cost-effective to retain in-house, to skilled and trusted out-of-house specialists.

TAKING DECISIONS ABOUT TECHNOLOGY

It is no longer a primary enabler to business, it is now a major driver of change. Understand how technology will radically affect the whole foundation of your business. As soon as one organization in your value chain moves to an e-business model, all partners must follow or risk being replaced by a competitor that is better prepared. Recruit the internal and external resources you need to help your decision making and to bring expertise to any areas in which your organization does not excel.

THINGS TO DO

1. Identify the core competencies on which you plan to concentrate.

2. Be ready to take decisions about technology.

3. Consult internal and external experts to define the areas of your system that need overhauling.

4. Make time to learn about e-business technologies.

MAKING CULTURAL CHANGES

The changes required by e-business do not stop at the strategic or structural levels but invariably involve the need to transform the culture of your organization. Recognize the value of retaining quality staff and provide on-going training and incentives.

15 Help staff to understand the possibilities the digital future offers.

Entrepreneurial

Independent

Self-starting

Dynamic

Flexible

QUALITIES OF GOOD STAFF

FOCUSING ON PEOPLE

If your organization is to cope with continual change, you will require staff who are ready to act as entrepreneurs, take risks, and act on their own initiative. You and your staff must be flexible and able to react quickly to identify new opportunities. Ensure your team is in a position to align strategy, technology, and processes to deliver superb customer value. Recruit staff who can fulfil these needs.

EDUCATING YOUR STAFF

Give your staff the opportunity to gain the skills necessary to manage in an e-business environment. Offer in-house training opportunities for staff so that they are in a position to undertake the changes to e-business. Look for a partner organization that can provide on-going technology intelligence and practical training to support your staff. Check their credentials and make sure they understand your market and can focus on changes that will have an impact on your organization.

▼ TRAINING STAFF
Educate your staff about the impact of e-business and digital markets and equip them with the necessary technical skills.

IT consultant gives employee one-to-one training

PROVIDING INCENTIVES

Make finding and retaining high-quality staff one of your highest priorities. E-business has created a major skill shortage in both technical and managerial positions. Technology experts have to cope with fast developments while managers struggle to translate technology-led marketplaces into money-making business strategies. Offer your staff incentives and make sure they feel they have a valuable role to play within your organization.

> **16** Show commitment to your staff, keep them well-informed, and reward their feedback and ideas.

CULTURAL DIFFERENCES

The use of incentives to retain and motivate staff varies across countries and industries. In the US, large rewards for success are standard, while in Japan employees are expected to be fully committed without extra incentives. In Europe, the UK is closer to the US model than most countries, but the situation is moving towards more performance-based rewards.

CONSIDERING STAFF INCENTIVES

REWARD	ADVANTAGE
SHARE OPTIONS Gift of shares or the option to buy shares.	Staff have a material reason to aim for the organization's success and are result-focused.
PERFORMANCE-RELATED BONUSES One-off payments related to performance.	Staff have an incentive to produce excellent results and work efficiently.
TRAINING Continual opportunities to learn new skills.	Staff will be more highly skilled and better able to handle the challenges of fast change.
FLEXIBLE WORKING CONDITIONS Working at home options and flexitime.	Staff feel trusted and the organization can retain staff that they might otherwise lose.
CAREER DEVELOPMENT The chance to move up the managerial ladder.	Staff are motivated to do well, knowing that good results will lead to promotion.
SALARY INCREASES A structure of basic pay increases.	Staff know that the improvement of their skills is reflected in their pay.

FOCUSING ON CUSTOMERS

The golden rule of e-business is that the customer is king. Focus on your customers and understand their needs so that you can put the appropriate customer-service processes in place.

CARING ABOUT CUSTOMERS

Your aim is to provide exceptional service for your customer. Understand that customers have immense choice and seek to create systems that allow one-to-one relationships, putting quality of service ahead of the expectation of making a sale.

 17 Focus all your efforts on creating the best customer experience.

THINGS TO DO

1. Keep an eye on new competitors.
2. Establish a way of monitoring existing and new competitors.
3. Identify your customers' needs and wishes.
4. Give customers access to the information they need.

UNDERSTANDING CUSTOMERS' CHOICE

In the days when your customers shopped exclusively on the high street, or purchased by telephone or mail order, their opportunity for direct comparison of price or features was limited. The Internet allows individual or business customers to make comparisons easily and complete their purchases from their own home or office. Many Web sites now exist solely for the purpose of enabling comparison shopping. Understand that power rests with the customer and put their needs at the centre of your business.

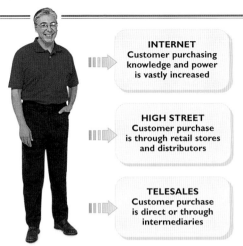

INTERNET
Customer purchasing knowledge and power is vastly increased

HIGH STREET
Customer purchase is through retail stores and distributors

TELESALES
Customer purchase is direct or through intermediaries

◄ **UNDERSTANDING CUSTOMER CHOICE**
The Internet has given customers access to comparative information on products and services on a global scale, far greater than that offered by retail, mail order, or telesale outlets. You have increased access to customers, but so do your competitors.

18 Put maximum effort into retaining valuable customers.

BUILDING A ONE-TO-ONE CUSTOMER RELATIONSHIP

In a situation where customers have so much choice and where many products and services cannot be differentiated on price or quality, caring for the customer has become the key point of differentiation. Avoid thinking of your customers as one or several broad groups. Focus on creating better customer relationships by tailoring customer communication according to the needs of each individual customer.

POINTS TO REMEMBER

● Customers expect a personal level of service.

● Customers should be treated on the basis of their own needs.

● It can cost up to ten times as much to gain a new customer as it can to retain an existing one.

● A one-size-fits-all approach to customer relationships does not work.

19 Ensure you and your staff are always in service mode before and after a potential sale.

MOVING THE SERVICE AHEAD OF THE SALE

Customer service traditionally begins after a sale. Start providing service from the moment of first customer contact. Eliminate the distinction between sales and service and focus on providing continuing, exceptional service. Attract customers by delivering excellent product information before the sale, and retain customers by building loyalty through after-sales service. Anticipate their needs by offering related products and services.

DELIVERING CUSTOMER NEEDS

Global competition has changed customers' expectations and the development of digital technologies has changed their experiences. Learn about the behaviour of your e-customers and respect their concerns about privacy and security.

20 Provide your customers with a faster service than your competitors.

21 Remember that time is money – integrate your processes to gain maximum efficiency.

FOCUSING ON DEMANDS

Customers increasingly demand fast service, quality goods or services, and competitive prices. Integrate your processes of search, selection, ordering, and fulfilment, to deliver the speed and efficiency that customers demand. The ability to check availability at time of order and make accurate fulfilment promises, together with an efficient packing and delivery system, is crucial to providing fast and excellent service.

BEING SENSITIVE

The development of e-commerce has increased the demand on individuals to release their personal details. Many organizations design their Web sites to gather data about potential customers as soon as they enter a site through mechanisms such as on-line forms. Be careful how you present these requests for information. Avoid upsetting potential customers by demanding too much information, especially if there are no apparent benefits to them. Answer potential concerns with a clear and easily accessible policy statement on your use of customer data and ensure this is consistent across all your customer service channels.

CULTURAL DIFFERENCES

Attitudes to privacy tend to vary between cultures, and laws governing data protection vary considerably between different countries. Be aware that you will potentially be dealing with customers in different legal systems, and with varying cultural expectations, and adjust your actions accordingly.

BEING SECURITY-AWARE

A major issue in the development of e-commerce has been the question of on-line security. Customers want the speed and flexibility of electronic transactions, but they also want to know that their data cannot be accessed by third parties. A failure of your data security could lose you customers very quickly. Seek to reassure your customers and implement the best security measures available.

QUESTIONS TO ASK YOURSELF

Q Have I identified the weakest element in my organization's security systems?

Q Have I sought the expertise of an external consultancy to inspect our security system and implement necessary changes?

Q Have I educated my staff to avoid security breaches?

22 Make your privacy and security policies clear.

23 Vet your own security systems for problems.

Consultant outlines security issues

▲ IMPLEMENTING SECURITY ISSUES
The human element is usually the weakest link in an organization's security system, but it is commonly ignored. Use an external consultant to brief staff on security procedures.

GIVING THE CUSTOMER ASSURANCES ABOUT SECURITY

Many individuals are understandably concerned about maintaining their privacy and security. Give customers the opportunity to decide whether you can share their data with third parties and give clear statements about your security safeguards.

❝ *It is just as safe to give bank details on-line as it is to give details to a shop assistant or over the telephone.* ❞

❝ *We have a responsibility to protect our customers in the event of a security breach.* ❞

❝ *We will refund any loss you may suffer resulting from any lapse in our security or our duty of care to you.* ❞

❝ *We will never release your details to another organization or person unless you give us permission.* ❞

ADDING CUSTOMER VALUE

The key aspect to e-business design is the need to redefine processes in terms of the value they offer the customer. Integrate your services so that your customer is in control, and ensure you deliver a consistently satisfying and individual experience.

24 Assess the total experience you deliver to your customers.

ENSURING GOOD CUSTOMER SERVICE

Most organizations focus on the price or quality of their products or services, but this is not sufficient when customers judge you on the total experience of doing business with you. Offer an excellent product or service, but also ensure that the experience of purchasing from you is the best that the customer can receive. Work to eliminate time-consuming, error-prone, or unsatisfactory customer service. Always consider the total experience and manage expectations by promising only what you are certain you can deliver.

◀ MONITORING CUSTOMER SERVICE
Put procedures in place to check that customer requirements are being met. Here, an electronic device records receipt of delivery, and sends confirmation to the customer database instantaneously.

DO'S AND DON'TS

✔ Do use customer self-service where possible.

✔ Do remember that competitors' products are easily available to your customers.

✔ Do always aim for higher standards.

✘ Don't give unrealistic delivery times.

✘ Don't allow any of your customer contact points to deliver unsatisfactory service.

✘ Don't rely on customer loyalty.

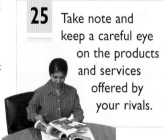

25 Take note and keep a careful eye on the products and services offered by your rivals.

TREATING CUSTOMERS AS INDIVIDUALS

Consumers regularly complain that they are made to feel unimportant and irrelevant by many businesses. Customers want to be treated as individuals and to be offered services personalized to their specific needs. Learn enough about your customers to be able to treat them as individuals. Build a detailed picture of each customer and ensure that this information can be accessed by all areas of your organization that come into contact with the customer. Tailor each customer interaction to the individual's needs.

26 Ask yourself how well you know your customers' individual needs.

▼ SHARING INFORMATION
All areas of your organization that come into contact with the customer must operate from a single customer database. Store a record of every contact with the customer, made through whatever channel.

Customer record is set-up on first contact

NAME Maria Anne Grant   REFERENCE 25 0124 005

ADDRESS 29 Hawthorne Road, Wells, Cheshire CH5 7GH

CONTACT 01558 225 669

Customer is assigned reference number to gain quick access to information

Each subsequent contact is entered on same log

17.02.00 - Customer contacted sales office to enquire about the possibility of purchasing book by mail order.

18.02.00 - Customer called to enquire about Web site address and methods of payments acceptable.

21.02.00 - Customer ordered three books on-line.

22.02.00 - Customer's order delivered.

All customer comments are recorded

INTEGRATING SERVICES

Effective e-business design requires you to identify all the processes within your organization that the customer comes into contact with and to use technology to integrate them for the benefit of your customers. This technology must be able to customize the sales and service experience for each individual customer. Extend integration beyond your own organization and share customer data with your supply-chain partners. Then you can achieve the level of service that is demanded by your time-conscious customers.

THINGS TO DO

1. Tailor selling opportunities according to the profile of each individual customer.

2. Build customer loyalty by creating a unique, personalized relationship.

3. Examine ways of integrating supply-chain partners.

SIMPLIFYING SERVICE

Be proficient at delivering a consistent quality experience irrespective of how the customer approaches your organization. Make it as simple as possible for the customer to get information, make a purchase, check delivery details, or get after-sales advice through all potential sales and service channels. Integrate all your service channels so that there is no perceptible difference between them in the eyes of your customers.

27 Take customer complaints seriously and act on them to improve your service.

28 Deliver fast, accurate, and helpful service.

29 Test the service your competitors offer customers.

ENSURING CONSISTENCY

Customers are quickly alienated when their details, complaints, or service history are not available to the representative dealing with them. Customers do not see why there should be a difference between the service they receive from you on the Web, in your retail premises, or over the telephone. Replace fragmented service with a reliable and consistent approach. Make sure your customers do not have to explain problems repeatedly to different people within your organization.

POINTS TO REMEMBER

● All staff who have customer contact should have easy access to the central customer database.

● Customer service must be consistent and reliable across every channel of communication.

● Your competitors will be working to gain your customers.

SHARING INFORMATION ▶
In this example, a customer asks a shop assistant if he can provide a product she has seen on the Internet. His response will determine customer satisfaction.

Product is not available in retail outlet

Customer asks sales assistant for a product advertised on Web site

GIVING THE CUSTOMER CONTROL

Frustrated by poor service, customers who value their time have embraced the opportunity for self-service that is offered by e-commerce. The ability to find information and order products or services on a 24-hour basis without having to deal with sales personnel has driven the take-up of e-commerce and has changed the face of entire industries. Implement self-service and benefit from lower costs, and fewer errors caused by multiple points of data re-entry.

30 Make customer contact points a top concern.

31 Benefit from the consumer taking control.

Satisfied customer receives product within 24 hours

Customer tracks delivery details of product from Internet at home

Sales assistant obtains product details and processes order

Sales assistant does not have access to Web database

Customer leaves dissatisfied

BUILDING ON
E-COMMERCE EXPERIENCES

The emergence of e-commerce has been the catalyst for IT solutions designed to enable the on-line, digital economy. Learn the lessons of e-commerce and use Internet technology throughout your organization, to give customers consistent service.

32 Review all your IT systems to ensure they work with e-commerce systems.

THINGS TO DO

1. Monitor the levels of speed and service through all your sales channels.

2. Critically assess your ability to deliver consistent customer experience.

3. Build business processes on sound and adaptable technological systems.

33 Recognize how the digital world affects customers.

34 Ensure your staff understand the full business picture.

LEARNING FROM E-COMMERCE

E-commerce has shown organizations the digital future. It has opened up a vision of an instant, global means of sharing information and has conclusively demonstrated that the customer must be the focus of e-business. Customers have demonstrated through their use of e-commerce that they judge organizations on the complete experience. They expect businesses to continually improve price, and to provide fast, accurate, personalized, and convenient service.

DO'S AND DON'TS

✔ Do ensure that every aspect of your business is focused on the customer.

✔ Do extend the technology of e-commerce throughout your organization.

✔ Do remember that customers will move to another supplier if they are not satisfied.

✘ Don't allow your traditional outlets to retain non-integrated technology systems.

✘ Don't concentrate on your Internet outlets to the detriment of your other outlets.

✘ Don't develop IT systems in isolation from your key business goals.

INTEGRATING DATA

The Web has seen the development of real-time systems in direct interaction with the customer, which deliver tremendous customer value. These systems are now essential tools in managing the customer experience, whatever the channel used to interact with your organization. Make sure your organization has effective on-line customer and product databases, while your stores, call centres, and field sales force can also access and benefit from the new and fully integrated systems.

35 Work from one customer database across all channels.

36 Constantly review the effectiveness of your IT systems.

Telesales force is in direct contact with customer and update customer database

Web site is continually monitored and database updated

Shop sales assistant has easy access to organizational and customer databases

Field staff can access product, customization, and delivery details, and place orders on-line

POINTS TO REMEMBER

● You should judge performance on how well you deliver the entire customer experience.

● You should aim to continually improve integration in all areas of your business.

● It is not enough to have effective on-line databases if the rest of your organization is not effectively integrated.

An e-business organization presents a fully integrated front to customers and creates satisfaction and loyalty

▲ INTEGRATING SYSTEMS

Customers expect your business to present a united front and provide consistent service, whether face-to-face, via the Web, by telephone, or through field staff.

DEVELOPING YOUR E-BUSINESS

Moving to e-business requires radical changes to business strategy, processes, and culture. Lead the practical development of e-business, and work to put integrated systems in place.

MANAGING CHANGE

The transformation to e-business requires your staff to face some new challenges. Sell the need to change, provide effective systems, implement on-going training, and motivate staff with good incentives to create a forward-thinking team.

37 Prioritize the changes required throughout your organization.

▲ **BRAINSTORMING**
Consider using external e-business visionaries to educate and enthuse staff through brainstorming sessions.

FACING THE CHALLENGE

The business world is undergoing continuous, rapid change. Darwin said that it is not the strong or intelligent who survive, but those who are the most responsive to change. Re-discover the entrepreneurial spirit and be prepared to destroy old ways of doing things in order to create new, dynamic alternatives. Expect to adjust the business model and operating strategies and processes constantly in response to changes in markets and in customers' needs. Develop new ways of thinking in this dynamic environment, so that new ways of behaviour can follow.

PRIORITIZING CHANGE

Every organization has particular strengths and weaknesses. It may not be possible to excel in all areas, but it is possible to outshine your competitors in narrowly focused areas that please your customers. Refine your focus according to your strengths and your customers' desires before prioritizing change. Focus on one of three qualities according to your market niche, your core competencies, and your customer interests:

● Deliver superb and accurate customer service.
● Deliver high-quality products or services.
● Offer irresistible and continual innovation.

Now prioritize change in the way that will best help you improve performance in your focus area.

38 Recognize your strengths and focus your energies on them.

39 Make sure you and your staff share the goals of your organization.

FOCUSING ON PRIORITIES FOR CHANGE

PRIORITY	BUSINESS ISSUES	FOCUS FOR CHANGE
SERVICE ● Personalized ● Pro-active ● Flexible	● Instant access needed for accurate customer details. ● Flexible response systems needed to fight off competition. ● Concentrate on the customer value proposition.	● Streamline customer-contact channels. ● Build cross-functional customer-related processes. ● Ensure suitable technology infrastructure.
PROCESS ● Efficient ● Low in cost ● Fast	● Efficient allocation of materials and resources. ● Share fast and accurate data with suppliers. ● Monitor processes to improve service and lower costs.	● Streamline internal information flows. ● Build an end-to-end process structure. ● Remove barriers between you and your suppliers.
INNOVATION ● Predict trends ● Listen to customers ● Create new products	● Manage continuous change and accept risks. ● Manage mergers and acquisitions for growth. ● Encourage entrepreneurship and forward-thinking.	● Create a robust and scaleable network infrastructure. ● Organize processes around your networks. ● Integrate with suppliers and partners.

SELLING CHANGE

Few people like change, yet the transition to e-business requires massive and continuing change both in the way we operate and the way we think about business. Help staff to comprehend fully the scale of the global business changes now taking place and show them the implications for your business and your industry. Lead change from the top and ensure staff feel directly involved in the decision-process and the implementation of the transformation of the business.

LEADING CHANGE ▶

Act as an evangelist for new business strategies and show that organizational change is being led from the top, while continuing to accept input from all levels.

POINTS TO REMEMBER

- Technology is the creator of change and the main enabler of the e-business concept.
- Understanding technology is no longer the preserve of the IT professional alone.
- All your staff must understand the concepts behind e-business systems and technologies.
- If your staff can see how technology reduces repetitive procedures, they are more likely to embrace change positively.
- Proficient staff should help other staff learn new technical skills.

DIRECTOR

Management works closely with senior directors

Director champions the implementation of e-business

Views and input from partners and external consultants are considered

MANAGER

Manager supports staff in embracing e-business concepts

Frontline staff give their ideas and feedback

STAFF

EMBRACING TECHNOLOGY

An e-business must be built on technology that streamlines and integrates processes. The target is the flow of information and ways to add value to it. Focus on your customer and partner relationships and become more responsive to the continuing need for change. Recognize that the implementation of technology for e-business is so entwined with business strategy and organizational structure, and so difficult to execute, that it should be embraced by all your staff, not just IT staff.

40 Recognize that your staff are your most valuable asset.

QUESTIONS TO ASK YOURSELF

Q Have I sold the need for business transformation effectively to my staff?

Q Have I offered the necessary on-going training opportunities?

Q Do my staff have the necessary support to implement changes to e-business?

Q Do I keep my staff informed about new procedures?

PROVIDING TRAINING

It is necessary to maintain the momentum for change after you have initially built up enthusiasm for it. If you want entrepreneurial and dynamic staff, support them with the necessary training. Implement a thorough, effective, and on-going programme to get you and your staff ready and able to make the changes you need. Instigate training for yourself and fellow managers to understand the business implications of e-business so you can work together to shape new strategies. Train operational staff to learn to use new technologies, since they will be using the systems on a day-to-day basis.

▼ UNDERSTANDING TECHNOLOGY

Reassure your staff about new technologies. Train them and yourself to understand and learn about new systems so that you are all in a position to evaluate the possibilities and implications for new business models and strategies.

Reassure	Train	Evaluate

BENEFITING STAFF

Explanations and training are essential to help your staff prepare for change, but you must also show staff how e-business can directly benefit them. Adapt your remuneration strategy to make your key staff partners in change. Concentrate on using networked applications to make work less repetitive, and to provide staff with on-line learning resources.

BENEFITS FOR STAFF ▶

Consider providing Internet access for staff who do not have this facility at home so that they can discover the benefits of using technology in their personal lives.

PLANNING FOR E-BUSINESS

The traditional methods for planning for the future have become out-dated in an e-business environment. Adopt a dynamic, continuous approach to planning and utilize constant feedback so that you can quickly adapt plans as business conditions change.

41 Ensure that planners work very closely with implementers.

42 Be prepared to discard developing projects quickly, if the direction of change shifts.

PLANNING ANALYTICALLY

Traditional businesses often use an analytically based planning approach to determine likely outcomes and to develop appropriate strategies. This process relies on analyzing historic data that may already be out-of-date. It can lead to problems in execution such as a lack of clear targets, or a failure to use feedback to modify strategies. Be aware that this approach is unlikely to deliver useful results in a fast-changing business environment.

PLANNING PRAGMATICALLY

A pragmatic approach to planning is often taken by large organizations. This relies on operational staff finding solutions to meet new, urgent needs. However, the communication of frontline staff's knowledge of imminent change to decision-makers is often too slow within hierarchical structures. This leads to projects being implemented to meet current needs, rather than thought out in terms of future strategies. If you are serious about e-business, adopt a more dynamic approach to planning.

43 Be prepared for a multitude of possible future developments and ensure you can respond quickly.

FORECASTING

In a stable business environment, forecasts can be developed by measuring past performances. However, in a rapidly changing and uncertain e-business world, past performance may bear little relation to future opportunities. In this situation, aim to create rather than predict the future. Define your desired outcome, then work backwards to identify the steps you need to take to achieve your goal.

USING CONTINUOUS DYNAMIC PLANNING

A continuous approach to planning allows you to make constant modifications, based on feedback. This helps remove the problems that frequently arise from the gap between planning and implementation. Set trigger points that initiate planned action when external factors meet a determined measure. Focus your centralized planning on aligning business processes with strategy and implementing a network infrastructure. Leave application selection in the hands of the frontline departments who will be using them.

44 Rely on feedback to plan effective strategies.

45 Continue to plan effectively even in a volatile business environment.

Senior Decision Makers

ORGANIZATIONAL PRIORITIES
● Assess customers' needs
● Evaluate capabilities
● Develop e-business strategy

EXECUTION BLUEPRINT
● Link business design to technology
● Draw up a business case
● Set technology infrastructure
● Set targets and frameworks

DEVELOPMENT AND IMPLEMENTATION
● Rapid prototype development
● Feedback
● Evaluation and refinement
● Deployment

Business unit, departmental staff, and IT staff

◄ **CONTINUOUS PLANNING**
This form of planning allows your organization to monitor the business environment continuously. You can then evolve your strategy through experimentation to find out what works and what does not. You can also foresee and respond to change quickly.

TRANSFORMING AN EXISTING BUSINESS

You need to make the transition to e-business before new, flexible competitors move quickly into your markets. Work with your staff to identify your customers' future needs, create an e-business strategy, and realign processes.

46 Stay in touch with present needs, while also planning for the future.

BUILDING YOUR TEAM

To plan an e-business transformation, you will require a cross-functional team that must include top-level executives. Your team should not be too large to prevent quick decision-making, but should include a mix of key operational and IT staff. Remember that the day-to-day business must continue to be run effectively while change is being planned. Employ good-quality assistants who can focus on running the business efficiently while you concentrate on delivering future success.

47 Employ external specialists to give the team guidance.

FORMING AN E-BUSINESS TEAM

PEOPLE	ROLE
SENIOR MANAGEMENT Chief Executives and Directors.	Top management must actively focus on and lead the move to e-business.
IT STAFF Senior IT managers and IT planners.	Senior IT staff can advise on enabling technologies that meet your business needs.
BUSINESS MANAGERS Representatives from units impacted by change.	Senior business managers work with IT managers to manage the teams and identify IT solutions.
PARTNERS Business and IT representatives of your organization's partners.	Key partners are involved to ensure integration with their processes and technologies.
CONSULTANTS Specialists in areas in which in-house skills are insufficient.	External specialists strengthen your team's skills. Do not allow them to run your project.

IDENTIFYING ROUTES

The input of your team is integral to transforming a business. Work together to form a strategy that explains what you plan to do and define what you intend to offer your customers. This is the starting point for your e-business design, which shows how you are going to evolve. Your e-business design identifies what internal or external processes you need and how they should be integrated.

48 Actively encourage suggestions from all your staff.

▼ **LISTENING TO STAFF**

Listen to your frontline staff, since they are in a position to identify beneficial routes or possible obstacles to change.

Sales manager explains her team's ideas and feedback

IT manager advises on technology issues

FOCUSING ON CUSTOMERS

Take the customer's needs as the starting point. Gather detailed knowledge about your customers and all trends that indicate how they and their needs are changing. Use any existing customer databases you may have – including customer questionnaires, focus groups, and consumer research – to help understand your customers and how you can deliver them measurable benefits.

49 Identify the specific future needs of your customers and focus on the ones you are best able to satisfy.

UNDERSTANDING EXISTING PROCESSES

Before you can identify the steps to an e-business structure, ensure you have a clear understanding of how your existing processes work. Rather than trying to examine all the processes at once, pick those that most directly impact on the value you intend to offer the customer. If superb customer service is the factor you will focus on, concentrate on identifying how all the processes that deal directly with the customer currently interact.

QUESTIONS TO ASK YOURSELF

Q What are we best at and what are we worst at?

Q How can we improve our current processes?

Q Is our use of technology led by IT or by business units?

Q What new capabilities do we need to be able to deliver value to our future customers?

50 Make sure you understand your target customers.

51 Look outside your industry for new, dynamic ideas.

SIMPLIFYING PROCESSES

Plan new ways of operating to simplify and speed up your business processes before turning your attention to the technology that will be needed to implement your new design. Remember that the e-business design process starts by focusing on customers and then works backwards to find the simplest, fastest, or most cost-effective process needed to deliver customer value. Integrate functions to achieve a seamless, end-to-end process. Consider outsourcing parts of your business if this will aid an effective solution.

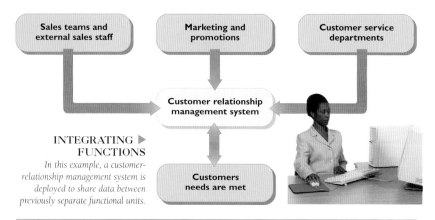

Sales teams and external sales staff

Marketing and promotions

Customer service departments

Customer relationship management system

Customers needs are met

INTEGRATING ▶ FUNCTIONS
In this example, a customer-relationship management system is deployed to share data between previously separate functional units.

IDENTIFYING TECHNOLOGY

With a new business design in place, consider which technology applications will best suit your requirements. Critically examine your existing use of technology and identify your strengths and weaknesses in this area relative to your proposed e-business strategy. Develop a technology blueprint to define the tools that will be used, how they will be integrated, and what costs and timescales will be involved. Aim for an infrastructure of open standards and Internet-enabled technologies.

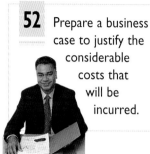

52 Prepare a business case to justify the considerable costs that will be incurred.

PRIORITIZING DEVELOPMENT

Many large-scale technology projects take more than a year in the planning, plus another year or more in their implementation. Large projects with long lead times are increasingly risky in times of rapid change because, if business needs change, the initiative may lose its relevance or importance before it can be implemented. Work with a technology supplier who can adapt to your needs. If a single initiative cannot be broken down into stages that can be implemented within the timescale, find an alternative approach.

53 Look at the technology used by your competitors.

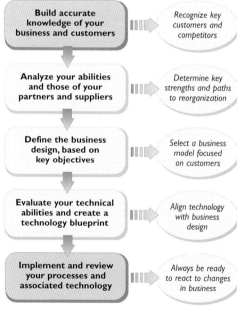

Build accurate knowledge of your business and customers → Recognize key customers and competitors

Analyze your abilities and those of your partners and suppliers → Determine key strengths and paths to reorganization

Define the business design, based on key objectives → Select a business model focused on customers

Evaluate your technical abilities and create a technology blueprint → Align technology with business design

Implement and review your processes and associated technology → Always be ready to react to changes in business

▲ FORMING AN E-BUSINESS DESIGN

Set targets that are quickly achievable. Plan your development in steps that can be achieved within a 3–6 month timescale. Aim to take small steps so that results and benefits can be quickly demonstrated to the organization and enjoyed by your customers.

UNDERSTANDING BACK-OFFICE SYSTEMS

The adoption of integrated back-office systems, or Enterprise Resource Planning (ERP) applications, is driven by the need to make businesses more efficient. Understand their importance and match system design to your e-business strategy.

54 View back-office systems as an essential foundation of your business.

55 Seek ways to integrate different functions into a single back-office application.

USING ERP SYSTEMS

Many organizations operate on disparate systems that cannot deliver real-time information and which are unable to communicate easily, if at all, with other IT systems in the organization. The growth of back-office systems, or Enterprise Resource Planning (ERP) systems, has come from the need to eliminate problems caused by multiple and disconnected software applications.

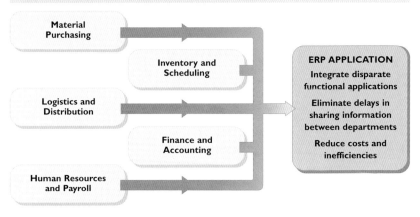

COMMON ELEMENTS OF AN ERP APPLICATION

Material Purchasing

Inventory and Scheduling

Logistics and Distribution

Finance and Accounting

Human Resources and Payroll

ERP APPLICATION

Integrate disparate functional applications

Eliminate delays in sharing information between departments

Reduce costs and inefficiencies

CREATING A FOUNDATION FOR E-BUSINESS

The move to e-business requires ERP systems to be integrated into other systems so that your entire value chain is streamlined. Make your ERP system the foundation for your e-business structure. Ensure seamless communication between ERP systems and other essential applications, such as customer-relationship management and supply-chain management systems. Recognize the benefits of systems using Internet standards, so that information can be shared easily between partners and suppliers.

56 Expect systems implementation to be complex.

57 Implement back-office systems that are fully Internet-enabled.

INTERNET-COMPATIBLE SOFTWARE

Since an ERP system must act as the foundations for an e-business structure, it is important that it can communicate seamlessly with other IT systems in the organization. Today's ERP systems make use of Internet standards to ensure that they are widely compatible with other systems, and to allow information to be shared and accessed easily. This need has resulted in a move towards Java-based software (a platform-independent programming language) that works in a standard Web browser. This means that users can gain access to their ERP system and corporate data from any networked computer with a normal Web browser.

POINTS TO REMEMBER

● You should select an ERP solution that matches your business strategy.

● You may encounter internal resistance when you plan changes to existing systems.

● Systems using Internet standards can communicate easily and share information effectively.

● The streamlining of processes should be led by your strategic needs, not your ERP system.

MATCHING ERP NEEDS WITH STRATEGY

Before picking an ERP system you must first determine what kind of organization you are planning to be in the digital future. Only choose an ERP system after you have created your e-business design. Business process re-engineering is an inevitable requirement when an ERP system is installed. However, try to avoid adapting your processes to fit the ERP software. Concentrate on the processes you need to streamline in order to reach your strategic e-business targets.

INTEGRATING IT SOLUTIONS

Many organizations have inherited IT systems that are incompatible with their newer systems. Examine your systems to understand how they developed and where information bottlenecks and barriers exist, and then begin to plan integration processes.

58 Identify how many incompatible systems your organization uses.

59 Seek out any bottlenecks of information.

60 Think about how your network may need to extend.

HOW SYSTEMS DEVELOPED

Computer hardware and software programmes, or applications, were developed to meet functional requirements, such as payroll, but these systems were typically unable to share data. Networks developed to connect systems with users but were often unable to connect to separate networks. The advent of the Internet brought a set of open standards (protocols) for communicating, storing, sharing, and transporting data, which finally created the opportunity to share information with any system or anyone, anytime and anywhere.

FINDING BOTTLENECKS

The secret to success in the digital business is to use Internet-aware networks and applications to eliminate information bottlenecks. Avoid a mix of old and new non-integrated systems, which tend to form islands of information within your organization. In this situation, information may be transferred between non-integrated systems by means of batch transfer of files at set times across a network, but this means that information is not available in real-time. Accept that the free-flow of information is a key part of your IT architecture.

QUESTIONS TO ASK YOURSELF

Q Do any departments have to transfer files to each other, or to suppliers, by disk?

Q Do any departments have to re-enter data manually?

Q Is everyone within the organization able to share real-time information?

Q Are there adaptable IT systems in place?

REMOVING BARRIERS

The goal is to streamline the end-to-end business process. Many organizations are faced with a mixture of systems and isolated, functionally based departments or business divisions. Recognize that replacing inherited systems is always difficult and expensive, and may be impractical. Some systems can be retained and adapted. Consider adopting integrating software, or "middleware", to transfer data between old and new systems.

STREAMLINING NETWORKS ▼

Identify and eliminate systems that are not integratable within your organization. Adapt systems that can be integrated effectively, and invest in the technology that will allow integration.

THINGS TO DO

1. Ask staff to identify information blockages.
2. Identify the limitations of your existing systems.
3. Eliminate redundant systems that cannot be integrated into a new business structure.
4. Identify the costs and time implications of integration.

Identify ▶ **Adapt** ▶ **Integrate**

▲ BUILDING AN E-BUSINESS STRUCTURE

The network services are the foundation of your e-business. Databases and applications rely on this, and create a path to your audiences and customers.

DEVISING A STRUCTURE

E-business architecture can be thought of as an inter-dependent layer of services. The network services are the infrastructure that forms the basis for various services such as file transfer, e-mail, and databases. These facilitate the business applications that form the next layer. The top layer comprises the interfaces used to communicate with your audiences, such as a public Web site, an Extranet for partners, and retail outlets. These gateways collect information from the business services in the layer below and present them to audiences in an appropriate form.

61 Use customer interfaces to identify and collect data and relay feedback to business services.

CREATING A NETWORK

Since e-business is built on the concept of networks, it is essential that your network is fast, robust, scalable, secure, and fully Internet-enabled. Your network must also have sufficient capacity for future increases in traffic. Ensure your network can be expanded as and when required without adding complexity, reducing flexibility, or disturbing any other part of the infrastructure. In the digital environment, your organization needs to work on Internet time, which means being available 24 hours a day. Remember that any network downtime is unacceptable.

QUESTIONS TO ASK YOURSELF

Q Have we defined the network standards we will support?

Q Have we ensured speed, robustness, and scalability?

Q What enabling technologies are available to us?

Q What key business applications shall we use to support our business process?

Q What information access will we offer our audience?

62 Ensure your systems are stable and will not fail.

63 Select an Application Service Provider partner with care.

BUILD, BUY, OR RENT?

A key issue for organizations moving to e-business is the decision to build, buy, or rent IT systems. Self-built systems can be expensive and difficult to improve. Building simple middleware applications to integrate old systems, may, however, be justified. Off-the-shelf systems should be Internet-aware and compatible with open standards. Consider leasing applications from Application Service Providers (ASPs). The applications reside at the ASP to which you connect via a secure Internet connection. This may allow you to outsource your technology needs, reduce costs, and retain flexibility.

MOVING OUTSIDE THE ENTERPRISE

Integrating systems within your organization is not enough – successful businesses must share their information seamlessly with partners and suppliers throughout the value chain. This requirement adds to the importance of adopting Internet standards, open systems, and a limited set of widely used enabling technologies. Ensure your systems can communicate easily with those of partners and suppliers. Retain the flexibility needed to change the organizations you work with according to evolving business requirements.

Key

◀▶ *Audience access*

◀▶ *Systems integration*

Suppliers and partners

Stakeholders

Supply-chain management systems

Management

Reporting and finance applications

Decision support systems

ENTERPRISE RESOURCE PLANNING
- Production
- Distribution
- Fulfilment

Employees

Sales-force management systems

Human resources and administration applications

Customer-relationship management systems

Resellers

Customers

◀ NETWORKED SYSTEMS

An effective e-business network links back-and front-office applications to allow a seamless flow of information. Each audience group then has access into the system and can gather the relevant information they need.

USING CUSTOMER-MANAGEMENT SYSTEMS

There has been a rapid growth in technological solutions for customer-relationship management (CRM). Understand the forces driving CRM systems and develop a suitable strategy that will ensure consistent service across multiple contact channels.

64 Design your infrastructure to be accessible to your business partners.

65 Remember that a 5% increase in customer retention can increase profits by over 75%.

WHY USE CRM?

As customers increasingly focus on the quality of service they receive, an effective customer-relationship management (CRM) strategy is essential for improving customer retention. CRM systems use a single source of customer data to feed one or more applications designed to support functional tasks such as ordering, sales, customer service, and marketing. Increasingly, they also enable the customer to select self-service through a Web site.

DEVELOPING CRM

Effective customer relationships are important for every e-business but their degree of importance will vary depending on your organization's strategic focus. If delivering superb service is your goal, then a powerful CRM system will be more essential than if your focus is on constant innovation. Once you have decided to embark on a CRM system, use your e-business design to identify the customer contact functions that are critical to your business. Remember that the introduction of a CRM system will inevitably require internal reorganization. Constantly communicate with the staff involved with the reorganization.

QUESTIONS TO ASK YOURSELF

Q Have I determined how the CRM system will help us achieve our strategic goals?

Q Have I evaluated the merits of different CRM systems, and considered the benefits of a purpose-built system?

Q Have I compared CRM systems from a variety of vendors to decide which is best?

Q Have I identified a list of our functional requirements for a CRM system?

BEING CONSISTENT

Whichever CRM system you choose, make sure that it will enhance the customer's experience of your organization, irrespective of which channel is used. It is not sufficient to have a CRM system linked to your Web site if your call centres cannot access the same database. The customer may be impressed by your service on the Internet, but will be quickly disillusioned if he or she does not receive the same standard of service from your store. Customers often research products through one channel before initiating a transaction through another. Ensure your CRM system is capable of seamlessly integrating information. Make use of digital contact technologies, such as WAP phones, iTV, and Kiosks to interact with your customers.

66 Consider only Internet-based CRM systems.

POINTS TO REMEMBER

● Each service channel must have immediate access to customer history and contact data.

● Digital contact devices offer new ways of accessing customers.

● Your sales personnel should determine the appropriate approach for each individual.

67 Provide strong leadership and overcome internal resistance when introducing a new CRM system.

▲ STAGES OF A
CUSTOMER LIFECYCLE
A CRM system must support all three stages of a customer lifecycle – acquiring a customer, improving the relationship, and retaining their loyal custom.

EXPLAINING NEW CONTACT TECHNOLOGIES

KEY TERM	DEFINITION
WAP Phone	WAP (wireless application protocol) mobile phones allow users to connect to the Internet, receive e-mail, and browse WAP-enabled sites.
iTV	Digital, interactive television marries broadcast television and the Internet, allowing advertisers to exploit the best of both media.
Kiosk	Kiosks are easy to use, often touch-screen, computers sited at point-of-sale or enquiry locations to give customers a self-service option.

USING SALES-FORCE MANAGEMENT

The needs of e-business are driving the introduction of sales-force management (SFM) systems. Assess the needs for a sales-force management system and set definable goals before creating an appropriate process and its supporting technology.

68 Look for opportunities to co-ordinate sales teamwork.

69 Cut down on re-entry of data, as it takes time and can introduce mistakes.

DEFINING SALES-FORCE MANAGEMENT

Sales-force management (SFM) is the integration of the often-separated functions involved in moving from a customer's initial inquiry to order-taking. This process typically includes pricing and quoting, confirmation of availability, or allocating commission payments. Introduce applications to integrate the separate functions into an end-to-end process, which seamlessly connect to CRM and ERP systems for maximum performance.

CO-ORDINATING SALES

The aim of sales-force management is to streamline the sales process in order to increase sales-force effectiveness and meet customer requirements. For example, your external sales staff may be operating in a number of different countries and cultures, but must tailor products to meet local requirements. Ensure information is readily accessible to your sales staff, wherever they are.

ACCESSING AND INPUTTING ▶
Give your sales staff the ability to access and input information from contact devices such as laptops and WAP phones, so that they can service customers' needs, even when they are travelling.

CASE STUDY

A major supplier of networking components was quick to adopt e-business strategies and solutions. As part of their move to e-business, the organization implemented a sales-force management system on-line, to eliminate typical manual processes that were both inefficient and error-prone. Implemented in phases, the system comprised a suite of networked commerce agents, which enabled resellers to configure, price, route, and submit electronic orders directly on-line. They started small by deploying an order-status agent, and then added pieces to the commerce suite. This suite was expanded to include a pricing and configuration agent, order placement, and invoice agents. As a result of developing the system, the organization cut the error-rate for order processing from 20% to 2%.

◀ **GAINING EFFICIENCIES**
In this case study, a leading organization was quick to see the advantages of streamlining its sales processes. The benefits of increased efficiencies were quickly seen after an on-line sales-force management system was implemented.

CREATING SFM SYSTEMS

The proliferation of channels available to the customers, the rise in self-service, and the increase in product customization means that the sales process is highly complex and often fragmented. First integrate this process by identifying every step required in the sales process for each important customer group. Look at the process from your customers' viewpoints and check that it meets their needs. Form a cross-functional team drawn from all departments involved in the process. Now identify those steps that are responsible for delays or inaccuracies in acquiring and processing an order.

FINDING AN SFM SOLUTION

DEFINE
Outline an end-to-end process that streamlines sales activity

→ Aim to work off centralized databases

DESIGN
Eliminate unnecessary steps and allow a free flow of information

→ Provide access to data via a Web browser interface

IDENTIFY
Find technology solutions that give sales teams access to data

→ Include tools such as on-line product customization

IMPLEMENT
Integrate individual functions into a streamlined process

→ Link seamlessly to back-office ERP systems

USING OUTSOURCING SUCCESSFULLY

The rapid growth in outsourcing has occurred because organizations are struggling to cope with the demands on their skills. Identify core competencies, create new partnerships to deliver needed skills, and learn to manage these vital relationships.

70 Increase flexibility by working with more than one outsourcer.

71 Look at every part of your business in your evaluation.

OUTSOURCING SKILLS ▼
Many organizations outsource key functions, such as accounting and IT services, once they have determined that these functions are not a core skill, and can be done more efficiently by out-of-house specialists.

ANALYZING STRENGTHS

The first step to identifying whether outsourcing is viable for your organization is to identify your core skills. Focus on your competitive edge and define what differentiates you from competitors. Look at those areas where others may be able to do the job better, faster, or cheaper than you. Even if you are a manufacturing business, your manufacturing skills may be less important than your brand management abilities. You could increase efficiency by outsourcing manufacturing and focusing on managing your brand.

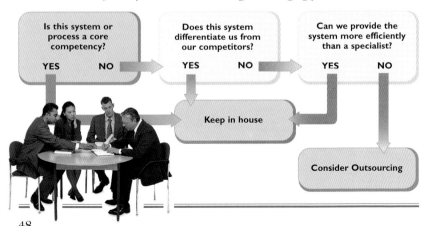

Is this system or process a core competency?
YES   NO

Does this system differentiate us from our competitors?
YES   NO

Can we provide the system more efficiently than a specialist?
YES   NO

Keep in house

Consider Outsourcing

CREATING SUCCESSFUL PARTNERSHIPS

Once you have decided which, if any, functions can be outsourced, select an organization with whom you can develop a close partnership. Select organizations whose competencies can enhance your business and whose systems can be integrated with your own with minimum disruption. Your partners must be integrated so tightly with your organization that they become indistinguishable to your internal or external audiences. Define the commercial relationship and tailor rewards to the accurate delivery of services.

72 Create competition for your contract between rivals.

THINGS TO DO

1. Set performance targets and make rewards dependent on performance.

2. Negotiate short-term contracts, rather than long-term ones.

3. Retain flexibility to allow a change of partners when circumstances dictate.

73 Provide sufficient staff and resources to manage the outsourcing relationship effectively.

MANAGING OUTSOURCING

The success or failure of outsourcing will depend on the degree to which your organizations can learn to think and act as one. Achieving this ideal requires active relationship management. Pick managing staff who have good communication skills because they will act as the crucial link between internal system users and your suppliers. Ensure staff are trained in managing external relationships before implementing the changeover and carefully monitor performance and feedback.

▼ **MEETING REGULARLY**
Regular meetings with outsourcers should take place to ensure projects are progressing well. Build a management team with good interpersonal skills.

Sales manager outlines customer perspective

Outsourcing manager explains issues

STARTING A NEW E-BUSINESS

In many ways, the start-up e-business has an easier task than the existing business that has to transform old methods. Take advantage of recent rapid changes, clearly focus on customer value, identify your core skills, and choose beneficial business partners.

74 Fully research your target customers before starting a new venture.

75 Benefit from a clean slate and the ability to design systems from new.

STARTING FROM NEW ▼
The Internet allows a new organization to research existing offerings quickly, plan a unique strategy, and then implement it.

RESPONDING TO CHANGE

The rapid change to a digital environment is causing problems for many existing businesses, but, for new organizations, it offers enormous opportunity. Your start-up organization has the ability to design effective systems without the hindrance of inherited systems. Define a value proposition for your potential customers, unhindered by current customer perceptions or complicated commercial relationships with partners.

Research ▶ **Plan** ▶ **Implement**

RESEARCHING ON-LINE

The Internet is the perfect tool for rapidly conducting wide-ranging research into the market of your chosen value proposition, and gaining insight into your existing competitors. Use the Web to explore details of your competitors' offerings and pricing, and use newsgroups and other discussion forums to identify the wishes of potential customers.

76 Focus on delivering exceptional customer service within your chosen niche market.

FOCUSING ON A NICHE VALUE PROPOSITION

If an opportunity exists within any industry to significantly add value for customers, then there is a niche that a new e-business can fill. Your aim is to create an e-business design that offers an enhanced value proposition to your target audience and which consistently delivers, or exceeds, customers' expectations. Carefully tailor your offering to the niche you have identified rather than adopting a wide focus in the hope of attracting a larger audience. Before settling on the niche you will attack, make sure you answer all the searching questions you raise.

QUESTIONS TO ASK YOURSELF

Q Who are my target customers and how well do I know them?

Q How do I get and retain customer loyalty?

Q Who are my existing and possible future competitors?

Q How will my product or service reach the customer?

Q What are our core competencies?

Q How will technology continue to change the marketplace?

DIFFERENT TYPES OF ON-LINE VALUE PROPOSITION

BUSINESS MODEL	VALUE PROPOSITION FOR CUSTOMER
INFOMEDIARY	Provides a one-stop shop for all the information required in a specific area by a customer. Offers ease of use, quick results, and cost savings.
TRANSACTION INTERMEDIARY	Provides a unified process for finding, comparing, selecting, and purchasing products or services on-line. Offers speed and cost savings.
CATEGORY LEADER	Becomes a market leader by identifying a new value proposition and constantly innovating the customer experience. Offers the best total customer experience.
COMMUNITY CENTRE	Creates a topic-specific meeting place on-line where members can interact to share ideas and information. Offers ease of contact and community membership.
INDUSTRY PORTAL	Provides a single, easy-to-use facility for organizations within a specific industry to conduct business-to-business trading. Offers time and cost savings and access to new suppliers.

IDENTIFYING YOUR AIMS

Early dot-com businesses worked on the principle of rapid growth, financed by early investors, and aimed at building a large customer base. This was used to justify high valuations that would enable the business to move rapidly to an initial purchase offering. Some valuations could not be justified and markets now have more realistic expectations. Before embarking on your e-business design, clarify your business aims. Are you building a business for the long-term or is this venture one that you expect to sell in a short time?

77 Make sure you know who your competitors are.

78 Carefully assess potential threats to your proposed business model.

BUILDING A BUSINESS COMMUNITY

As a start-up, it is very likely that you will not have all of the skills needed within your organization. Decide on the core competencies you need in-house, then look for organizations that you can partner to acquire the skills, functions, and infrastructure that you require. Research electronic business communities (EBCs), which bring outsourcing partners together in a flexible arrangement that can be altered relatively easily as your needs change.

◄ OFFERING NEW VALUE

This case study shows that even market-leading organizations in very established and low-margin industries can be vulnerable to attack from a small start-up business that successfully identifies and delivers an innovative value proposition.

CASE STUDY

A start-up organization, built on e-business principles, took on real-world market leaders in the bookselling world by identifying and aggressively pursuing a new customer value proposition. A powerful ingredient in the new organization's ability to rattle the market leaders was the recognition that it could use technology to add new value to the book-buying public's shopping experience. The organization innovated the book browsing, selection, and buying experience and carefully managed its customers' expectations to achieve new levels of customer satisfaction. It focused on its core competencies and built an electronic supplier community to enable it to take on the heavyweight market leaders. In doing so, it raised customer expectations to a new level that its competitors had to struggle to meet.

RAISING PROFILES

A small organization can have a big presence in the virtual world without the cost of premises. However, one of the biggest challenges you face is the ability to attract sufficient potential customers to your Web site. Promoting yourself on-line may go largely unnoticed. Recognize that real-world advertising will probably be a very significant part of your start-up budget. Seek unpaid advertising through editorial coverage and use your EBC partners' presence in their own markets to extend the reach of your promotions.

▲ **ADVERTISING PRESENCE**
Real-world advertising, such as sponsorship, will help increase customer awareness of your presence. Look for innovative ways of advertising your presence.

79 Extend your market presence in the real world.

80 Allocate resources to promotion in the real world.

OPERATING IN THE REAL WORLD

Most new e-businesses operate exclusively in the on-line world, since this offers lower costs and easy access to customers. However, a physical presence can extend your reach. Consider creating a real-world presence by partnering a retail organization. A shop-within-a-shop scenario could offer a low-cost entry in key geographic locations and give you an edge over your competitors. Make sure your customer interface in the real world is linked to the same data as your on-line operation.

BRINGING IN A WEB-CONSULTANT

Your public Web site and private Intranet site will be crucial elements in your new business design. Unless you have excellent Web development skills in-house you will need to work with a consultant or supplier to design and build your sites. Take the time to carefully research a suitable supplier. Make sure that the brief you supply is comprehensive and look at previous examples of their work to ensure that they are capable of creating the type of Web presence you need.

LOOKING AT E-MARKETING

Marketers must adapt the techniques they use for broadcast messages, via television, to narrowcast communication, such as via the Web. Understand how you can use e-media marketing techniques and look for opportunities for new promotions.

81 Use on-line sponsorship to reach potential customer groups.

THE FOUR PS

Product – spot emerging trends to offer continuous innovation

⬇

Price – innovation or added value can justify premium price

⬇

Place – customers are targeted through multiple channels

⬇

Promotion – shift to focus on a one-to-one approach

REAPPLYING MARKETING

The classic elements of marketing, the four Ps - product, price, place, and promotion – still apply to e-marketing, but they must be re-examined within the context of the new digital environment. In a world where it is increasingly difficult to differentiate products by price, identify how you are adding new value for the customer. Segment your customer base to use effectively the unique targeting abilities offered by e-media.

82 Use a mix of on-line and off-line promotion, but ensure they both use consistent images and messages.

MARKETING THE BRAND

The value of a strong and trusted brand image is crucial to differentiate you from your competitors and encourage customer loyalty. Brands that are already leaders in the physical world have an advantage provided that they can successfully translate their brand values to the on-line world. If your brand exists solely on-line, create awareness among your target audience, and portray messages that reflect your brand values.

POINTS TO REMEMBER

● The on-line medium is more suited to target marketing, rather than mass-marketing.

● Test advertising banners on Web sites that attract large numbers of your target customers.

● You should consider developing demographic and psychographic profiles of your targets.

GETTING AHEAD

The interactive and focused nature of digital media means that direct marketing techniques are ideal for one-to-one marketing on-line. Conduct direct marketing campaigns on-line and benefit from the ability to measure, in close to real time, the effects of changes to copy, placement, and other variables. Test and refine targeted offerings to key audience groups.

83 Use your Web site to build customer e-mail lists for use in direct marketing campaigns.

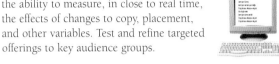

BENEFITING FROM ON-LINE PROMOTIONS

MEDIA	ACTIONS TO TAKE
WEB SITE	Study leading Web sites for lessons on design and presentation. Keep loading times low and tailor the presentation to support users with older browsers. Analyze the use of your site constantly.
E-MAIL	Encourage customers to register with you in order to receive news and updates via e-mail. Only send e-mails to customers who have chosen to receive them. Use e-mails for direct marketing.
ON-LINE ADVERTISING	Segment your audience, then pick sites that attract your potential customers. Constantly test and refine all aspects of your adverts including copy, size, media property, position, and offering.
ON-LINE SPONSORSHIP	Use sponsorship to build relationships with key target audiences. Sponsor sites that attract your targets. Reinforce leads generated by sponsorship with advertising and direct marketing.
COMMUNITIES	Identify on-line communities whose interest area attracts your target customers. Do not alienate users by an overtly commercial approach. Be open when dealing with queries about your products.
MOBILE PHONES	Send customers news and updates via digital mobile phones with the ability to connect to Web-based data. Ensure the content is tailored to small display screens.
INTERACTIVE TV	Allow users access to Web-based data and e-mail via digital, interactive TV. Using click-through links from programmes to suppliers' Web sites, reach customers via their lifestyle interests.

GETTING CLOSER TO SUPPLIERS

The opportunity to improve the supply chain is an important benefit of e-business. Drive supply-chain transformation and gain savings, greater flexibility, and enhanced customer value.

UNDERSTANDING E-SUPPLY

Supply chains vary considerably depending on the size and type of business, but, whatever the set-up, streamlined processes offer the best benefits to the end-customer. Understand your supply chain and learn how to transform it for e-business.

84 Identify the steps your products take before they reach your customers.

A SIMPLE SUPPLY CHAIN

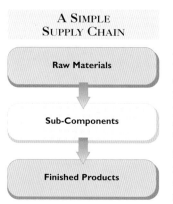

Raw Materials

Sub-Components

Finished Products

DESCRIBING THE SUPPLY CHAIN

An organization's supply chain is the system that produces the finished products needed to service customers. It invariably consists of several interdependent relationships with suppliers and partners that assist in the sourcing, manufacturing, storage, and distribution of products or services. The supply chain is responsible for adding value to physical goods by taking raw materials and manufacturing, assembling, and distributing them as a finished product. Remember that the chain must also facilitate the flow of information.

FOCUSING ON REQUIREMENTS

Many organizations have concentrated solely on reducing costs in their supply chains. In your e-business, focus on your customers' needs. Deliver what your customer wants, when they want it, and where they want it. Be able to fulfil their demands rapidly and cost-effectively. Aim to improve responsiveness and shorten order cycle times. Ensure you have the support of your supply-chain partners in your aims.

ASSESSING YOUR SUPPLIERS

The increase in outsourcing and the development of tightly integrated electronic business communities (EBCs) are being driven by the urgent need to streamline and integrate all the elements of a supply chain. Suppliers vary from those already using e-business systems, to those for whom integrating IT systems is still a remote ideal. Define the ways in which your partners' systems should integrate with yours and shortlist only suppliers who have the will and the technical abilities to meet your needs.

◀ **SUPPLY-CHAIN ELEMENTS**
The elements of the supply chain are frequently separate entities that co-operate to transform raw materials or components into finished products for distribution to your customer. Along with moving materials and products, the supply chain must also be adept at moving information.

Suppliers → Manufacturers → Warehousing → Distributors → Resellers → CUSTOMER

DO'S AND DON'TS

✔ Do recognize that you need the support of your suppliers.

✔ Do work to bind your supply chain together.

✔ Do ensure information flows between all your suppliers and partners.

✘ Don't underestimate the importance of an integrated supply chain.

✘ Don't neglect any one element of your supply chain.

✘ Don't stop monitoring supply-chain processes.

85 Look for the bottlenecks in your supply chain and ensure information moves efficiently.

INTEGRATING THE SUPPLY CHAIN

*O*rganizations can no longer work in isolation and must examine their supply chains for opportunities for integration. Understand the benefits of supply-chain management and re-engineer your supply chain to remove barriers to information.

86 Understand that information is as important an asset as inventory.

87 Good relationships with partners lead to a better chance of retaining customers and reducing costs.

MANAGING SUPPLY

Each typical key activity within a supply chain is often handled by separate organizations. The purpose of supply-chain management (SCM) is the co-ordination of the flow of information, money, and materials between all the organizations in the chain. Consider adopting Internet-enabled SCM to achieve efficient relationships with your partners, reduce costs, and, more importantly, provide competitive advantage in the battle to win and retain customers. Recognize that it is competition between business communities rather than between individual organizations that is changing the face of many industries.

◀ **OPERATIONAL EXCELLENCE**
In this example, a computer business used supply-chain management to integrate suppliers into a flexible supply chain that quickly delivered high-quality, customized products at reasonable prices.

CASE STUDY
A computer business identified its best customer value proposition as building top-quality but inexpensive computers and delivering them quickly to the end customer. This required the organization to focus on delivering operational excellence through the creation of an end-to-end process that integrated demand from the sales chain with a flexible supply chain. The organization became one of the leaders in developing SCM solutions to enable it to offer customers a fast and efficient build-to-order service. It recognized that a key supply-chain requirement was the ability to respond quickly to continual changes in customer demand. The Web-based customer interface became crucial for delivering real-time demand data, while allowing customers to customize orders on-line, and check their order status through to final delivery.

REMOVING BARRIERS

Aim to eliminate any barriers to information in your supply chain. This requires optimization of the whole, end-to-end process rather than the traditional approach of optimizing processes within a single organization. Until recently, it was almost impossible for an organization to gather sufficient information to synchronize their entire supply chain, so the chain often carried expenses such as incorrect stock levels. Implement Internet-enabled SCM systems to eliminate information barriers between you and your supply-chain partners.

INTEGRATED SUPPLY CHAIN
Suppliers, manufacturers, warehousing, distributors, and resellers use an internet-enabled **SCM** database

CUSTOMER
benefits from efficient results and is more likely to reward you with custom

▲ FULLY INTEGRATED
Use internet-enabled SCM to eliminate inter-organizational barriers, share data, and streamline entire processes.

88 Ask yourself if your supply chain causes poor customer service and look for SCM solutions.

POINTS TO REMEMBER

- If your supply chain is not integrated, it can lead to poor levels of customer service and non-optimal stock levels.
- An SCM system must be integrated with ERP systems.
- ERP systems are a useful research database for SCM planners.

PLANNING AND IMPLEMENTING SCM

Planning and execution are the two key elements of SCM. They are often poorly related in businesses that do not have integrated SCM. Undertake these elements collaboratively with supply-chain partners. Your SCM system should eliminate the gap between planning and execution for all your partners, and allow for continual adjustments to your processes using real-time data from the chain.

ELEMENTS OF AN SCM SYSTEM

PLANNING	DATA	EXECUTION
● Demand Forecasting	Information must be available in real-time to all partners and suppliers in the supply chain	● Product Management
● Fulfilment		● Warehousing
● Transportation		● Replenishment
● Manufacturing		● Distribution
● Scheduling		● Reverse Logistics

ENSURING FULFILMENT

*E*fficient fulfilment means delivering *your promises on time. Work with your supply-chain partners to give accurate fulfilment promises. Allow customers access to delivery status and keep them fully informed throughout the fulfilment process.*

89 Make fulfilment a primary goal of your integrated supply chain.

90 Set fulfilment targets and then track performance.

91 Always aim to exceed customer expectations.

ACHIEVING PROMISES

Few things are guaranteed to upset customers more than a failure to deliver goods or services at the promised time or date. The ability to give accurate promises at the time of order is critical to efficient fulfilment, yet it can only be achieved if you have access to accurate, real-time information. Make sure that your SCM system allows you to constantly and accurately update demand forecasts and calculate accurate delivery promises. Ensure that the promises you make have a safety margin for any problems that may occur.

KEEPING CUSTOMERS INFORMED

Customers should be able to access details of their order, check its status, and confirm delivery through whatever point of contact with your organization – store, Web site, call centre, or kiosk – that they prefer to use. This means that you must be able to give customers access to information that may be held by other organizations in your supply chain.

Customer checks delivery details on Internet

GIVING CUSTOMERS ACCESS ▶
Ensure your Web site links data from all your supply-chain partners and allows your customers to gain access easily to order details.

THINGS TO DO

1. Align your supply-chain partners with your strategy.

2. Ensure supply-chain partners are focused on customers.

3. Train team members in interpersonal skills and business issues needed for collaborative partnerships.

WORKING WITH PARTNERS

Aim to work collaboratively with your suppliers and partners. Think and act as one extended enterprise focused on efficiently delivering a specific form of customer value. This requires new ways of thinking and excellent business, communication, and inter-personal skills. Work to create a project team, led by a senior executive, to manage supply-chain reorganization and integration. This team, together with their equivalents from your partners, will be responsible for integrating the entire supply chain.

MANAGING RELATIONSHIPS WITH PARTNERS

MANAGER
Be responsible for ensuring that your team, partners, and suppliers are working towards the same aims and that information is shared and free-flowing at all levels.

TEAM MEMBERS
Train your team members to be responsible for liaising with partners to reorganize and automate the supply chain.

PARTNERS
Treat your partners as an equal part of your business team. Work together to avoid any conflict of interests.

SUPPLIERS
Encourage communication and avoid behaving like the "customer". Accept suppliers as an extension of your business.

92 Use e-mail to confirm order and delivery details to customers.

DO'S AND DON'TS

✔ Do give convenient delivery-time options to customers.

✔ Do allow for delays when ensuring that promises can be met.

✘ Don't direct customers to a separate Web site for delivery details.

✘ Don't make Web site access time-consuming or complicated.

IMPLEMENTING SCM SYSTEMS

Supply-chain management (SCM) implementation is critical to the success of your e-business. Work with your partners to define issues, identify solutions for streamlining processes, make a business case for change, and manage the transformation.

93 Only consider SCM applications that are fully Internet-enabled.

POINTS TO REMEMBER

- You should understand your organization's strategy and e-business design before embarking on an SCM planning process.
- Your e-business design should describe how your supply chain must service customers.
- You should seek suppliers who are ready to adopt e-business practices and technology.

GETTING STARTED

Aim to merge functions inside your organization and across the supply chain to achieve greater efficiencies. Inherited supply-chain applications may not have been designed to work with other systems. Consider whether to replace all inherited systems at once or take a step-by-step approach. Remember that no single organization or decision-maker owns or even fully comprehends the entire inter-organizational process that is to be streamlined.

DEFINING YOUR SUPPLY-CHAIN PROCESSES

Structure your supply-chain processes to reflect your e-business strategy and business design. Your e-business design defines the competencies you intend to keep in-house, and the services you plan to outsource. If you outsource a key element, such as manufacturing, so that you can concentrate on sales and marketing, your supply-chain requirements will change markedly.

Maintains good interpersonal skills

Asks searching questions

Understands whole picture

Understands shared goals

Respects opinions

▲ MANAGING INTEGRATION

A good manager has the qualities needed to lead change positively and is able to work constructively with partners and suppliers to identify the issues that need addressing.

CREATING AN SCM SOLUTION

Create an SCM project team and work closely with partners

⬇

Communicate with and educate your team and partners

⬇

Clarify SCM goals and audit the supply chain

⬇

Identify technology options and prepare your business case

⬇

Implement your ideas and new processes

⬇

Use feedback to monitor results and refine future actions

95 Examine the complete supply-chain process to find areas for cost-savings.

STREAMLINING PROCESSES

The goal of your SCM plan is to achieve a process that links all parts of the supply chain and allows all parties access to the information they need in as close to real-time as possible. Audit your supply chain to identify where non-essential activities take place. For instance, do you really need to swap purchase orders constantly with your suppliers? Can you share the data directly between each other's SCM or ERP systems?

94 Find examples of activities that are duplicated, repetitive, or redundant, and eliminate them.

QUESTIONS TO ASK YOURSELF

Q Have I identified areas where data is rekeyed unnecessarily?

Q Have I identified barriers to information?

Q Have I identified where costs could be reduced?

Q Have I understood why some SCM systems have not been successful?

Q Do I understand why SCM execution must be carefully managed?

Q Have I clarified the potential rewards of implementing SCM?

MAKING THE CASE

Construct a clear business case to justify the often-substantial investment in technology. Address both the strategic and bottom-line benefits that your solution will deliver. There are case studies on the Internet from leading organizations that were early adopters of Internet-enabled SCM. Many demonstrate excellent return on investment and improved customer service, and some demonstrate the possible pitfalls to be avoided.

COMMUNICATING WELL

Integrating the supply chain is a considerable undertaking that requires close and co-operative working by all partners if it is to be successful. Supply-chain reorganization will affect departmental and business unit divisions in all the partner organizations. Problems can occur if there is a lack of individual understanding or commitment to change. Communicate constantly with all parties impacted by the change. Expect to invest considerable resources in educating your staff, suppliers, and partners on the reasons for, and techniques of optimizing business processes.

96 Plan for on-going training initiatives to take place.

97 Monitor new processes and continually assess performance.

METHODS OF COMMUNICATING

Ensuring good communication between all parts of your supply chain can be difficult, especially if your partners and suppliers are on the other side of the world. Use your organization's Extranet as a key means of ensuring constantly updated information. Create a separate section on your Extranet to allow team members to share ideas or issues that need resolving, and use regular e-mail updates to keep everyone abreast of developments. On-line video conferencing is a useful way of bringing participants together without the need to travel to meetings.

CASE STUDY

A start-up organization in the fulfilment market built a systems infrastructure that was entirely Internet-based. As a business-to-business supplier, it decided to manage all its communications through its Extranet. The organization distributed order and inventory information, customer data, and shipping details via the Internet to its partners and customers, and also conducted fund transfers electronically. Because the organization did business via the Internet, its physical location was irrelevant to its customers and partners. This meant the organization could reduce overheads by locating in a low-cost area, without the risk of alienating customers. It ran the technology on which it relied through an outsourcing arrangement with a technology provider, who supplied full systems support remotely via the Internet.

◀ INTERNET-ENABLED
The global nature of the Internet, and its increasing speed and capacity, has had a huge effect on the choices open to businesses. Even key members of the supply chain, such as this specialist fulfilment organization, can be tightly integrated within your internal processes without needing to be located close to your business.

CHOOSING TECHNOLOGY

Ensure you, your partners, and your suppliers have the fundamental network and supporting technologies in place before you implement an SCM system. If these elements are in place, choose between an off-the-shelf (OTS) SCM system or a collection of smaller, tightly integrated applications. Increasingly, organizations are using smaller, Web-enabled applications working off shared databases to address issues, such as fulfilment.

USING FEEDBACK

It is easy to become so focused on supply-chain realignment that you forget its purpose. Always keep in mind that supply-chain changes are driven by the goal of delivering customer satisfaction. They are defined by the value proposition your e-business strategy has selected, and their success is measured by the extent that they have delivered value to the customer. Your customers are the best source of SCM performance data, so make sure you have the ability to collect and analyze their responses. Always be ready to adjust processes in response to feedback and changing environments.

THINGS TO DO

1. Use your Web site to monitor customer responses and feedback.
2. Ensure your CRM and SFM systems can relay feedback on process efficiencies.
3. Use feedback constructively to adapt systems and processes where necessary.

RESPONDING TO CUSTOMER FEEDBACK

Actively seek customer feedback and recognize that it is a key ingredient in refining the performance of your supply chain. Your customer will feel valued if they know their views are listened to and acted upon. Use phrases such as these to welcome and react to feedback:

Hearing your comments about our performance helps us to improve the service we give you.

How can we change our performance to ensure that your needs are met successfully in future?

Please let us know if any part of our product or service fails to meet your highest expectations.

How can we best resolve your complaint to ensure that you receive complete satisfaction?

SAVING MONEY WITH E-PROCUREMENT

Procurement refers to the process of acquiring the goods and services that keep an organization functioning, such as office equipment or travel. Adopt Web-based applications to provide a new approach to procurement and reap the benefits.

98 Recognize the cost savings available from automating procurement.

99 Give staff access to procurement on-line.

100 Integrate your procurement and back-office systems.

PUTTING EMPLOYEES IN CONTROL

Put procurement on-line on your corporate Intranet, and give your staff the benefits of self-service. Use Web-based procurement applications so that employees can access authorized suppliers' catalogues from within their own Intranet. If you retain control of supplier approval and on-line catalogues, then you can ensure corporate purchasing standards are followed.

DEFINING PROCUREMENT

The terms procurement and purchasing are often used as if they are interchangeable, but purchasing is only one part of procurement. Purchasing covers the buying part of the process but procurement also includes selection, authorization, and delivery. Paper-based procurement requires a series of forms and authorization, which take employees time to fill, chase, and process. Adopt e-procurement and give staff less paperwork and more time.

Employee accesses on-line catalogue

▲ **AUTOMATING APPROVAL**
Make sure that the ordering system allows staff to check availability and delivery details on-line and that it automates approval and purchase-order systems.

IMPLEMENTING E-PROCUREMENT

Make sure your purchasing team is empowered to manage the e-procurement implementation to ensure that employee controls are retained in the automated system. Install workflow systems that automate approval and authorization tasks according to each employee's level of authority. On-line systems allow you to give each employee a purchasing profile that controls the goods and quantities they are authorized to purchase.

101 Focus procurement systems on reducing order-cycle times and organizational overheads.

BENEFITS OF E-PROCUREMENT

Automate repetitive and time-wasting tasks

Employees have access to suppliers' catalogues on-line

Purchasing staff have time to negotiate better deals

Employees and organization benefit from efficiencies

REAPING THE BENEFITS OF E-PROCUREMENT

BENEFICIARIES	BENEFITS
ORGANIZATION	Significant cost savings are made from greater efficiency in the processes of procurement and the resulting greater employee productivity.
EMPLOYEES	Employees benefit from a reduction in repetitive tasks and increased time to focus on real business issues. They have convenient, simplified choices to make.
PROCUREMENT SPECIALISTS	They receive better purchasing information and are in a strong position to make good deals with e-procurement suppliers. They are able to manage supply more efficiently.
SUPPLIERS	They benefit from a loyal partnership with your organization and more efficient ordering systems. They therefore maintain an advantage over their competitors.

ASSESSING YOUR E-BUSINESS SKILLS

*E*valuate your readiness for e-business by responding to the following statements, marking the option closest to your experience. Be as honest as you can: if your answer is "never", circle Option 1; if it is "always", circle Option 4, and so on. Add your scores together and refer to the Analysis to see how you scored. Use your answers to identify areas of e-business that you should focus on for improvement.

OPTIONS

1 Never

2 Occasionally

3 Frequently

4 Always

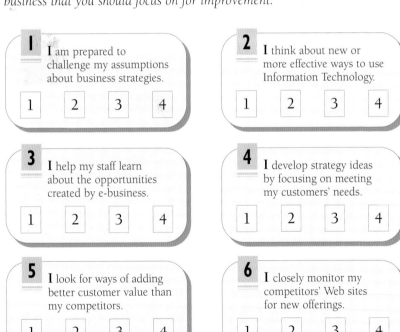

1 I am prepared to challenge my assumptions about business strategies.

1   2   3   4

2 I think about new or more effective ways to use Information Technology.

1   2   3   4

3 I help my staff learn about the opportunities created by e-business.

1   2   3   4

4 I develop strategy ideas by focusing on meeting my customers' needs.

1   2   3   4

5 I look for ways of adding better customer value than my competitors.

1   2   3   4

6 I closely monitor my competitors' Web sites for new offerings.

1   2   3   4

7 I encourage my staff to suggest and implement process improvements.

| 1 | 2 | 3 | 4 |

8 I utilize a dynamic planning method for e-business developments.

| 1 | 2 | 3 | 4 |

9 I make sure that my staff receive regular training to help cope with changes.

| 1 | 2 | 3 | 4 |

10 I look for ways to integrate separate functions into an end-to-end process.

| 1 | 2 | 3 | 4 |

11 I focus on ensuring that we know and fulfil our customers' expectations.

| 1 | 2 | 3 | 4 |

12 I look for ways to make our supplier relationships more effective and less costly.

| 1 | 2 | 3 | 4 |

ANALYSIS

Now you have completed the self-assessment, add up your total score and check your performance by referring to the corresponding evaluation. Whatever your level of e-business skills, remember that technology and the resulting business opportunities move on rapidly, and you must make an effort to keep in touch with new developments. Identify your weakest areas, and refer to the relevant sections in this book for guidance and advice.

12–24: Your e-business skills are quite limited: work on developing them if you are to benefit yourself and your organization.

25–36: You have a sound grasp of many e-business issues: review your weaker areas to improve those skills.

37–48: Your understanding of e-business is good: focus on continually keeping up-to-date.

INDEX

ACKNOWLEDGMENTS

AUTHOR'S ACKNOWLEDGMENTS

It takes much more than a manuscript to create a book and many thanks are due to the editors and designers at Cactus and Dorling Kindersley for their enthusiasm and professionalism in producing this book. Thanks are also due to Cisco, Sun, and Oracle for ideas and case studies. I also wish to thank my friend Tim Burman whose lovely ship, Bølgen, provided a perfect haven for writing, and whose dog Sam made sure I got up in the mornings!

PUBLISHER'S ACKNOWLEDGMENTS

Dorling Kindersley would like to thank the following for their help and participation:

Editorial Daphne Richardson, Mark Wallace
Indexer Hilary Bird; **Proofreader** Polly Boyd; **Photography** Gary Ombler.

Models Roger André, Philip Argent, Clare Borg, Angela Cameron, Kuo Kang Chen, Russell Cosh, Roberto Costa, Felicity Crowe, Patrick Dobbs, Carole Evans, Vosjava Fahkro, John Gillard, Ben Glickman, Kate Hayward, Richard Hill, James Kearns, Janey Madlani, Zahid Malik, Frankie Mayers, Sotiris Melioumis, Karen Murray, Mutsumi Niwa, Kiran Shah, Lois Sharland, Lynne Staff, Suki Tan, Peter Taylor, Ann Winterborn, Gilbert Wu, Wendy Yun; **Make-up** Jane Hope-Kavanagh.

Picture researcher Jamie Robinson; **Picture librarian** Melanie Simmonds

PICTURE CREDITS

The publisher would like to thank the following for their kind permission to reproduce their photographs:
Key: *b*=bottom; *c*=centre; *l*=left; *r*=right; *t*=top
Allsport: Clive Mason 53tr;
Corbis UK Ltd: R W Jones 4;
Robert Harding Picture Library: 31br;
Tony Stone Images: 10br; Christopher Bissell 28bl;
Telegraph Colour Library: 46br;
UPS: 22cl

AUTHOR'S BIOGRAPHY

Steve Sleight is an author and independent consultant with a background in writing, broadcasting, and communications. He has advised several prominent international companies on communications strategies as well as the use of IT and digital, interactive media to enhance their projects. Most recently, he has been developing an e-business approach to information publishing and he is now concentrating on producing digital, multimedia content that can be presented and delivered in traditional or new media forms. He writes on business subjects as well as on his real, all-consuming passion, sailing. He is the author of the *Essential Managers: Information Technology* as well as the DK *Complete Sailing Manual*.